Sled Dogs

by Joyce Markovics

Consultant: Helen Lundberg, President
International Federation of Sleddog Sports
Willow, Alaska

BEARPORT
PUBLISHING

New York, New York

Credits

Cover and Title Page, © iStockphoto/Thinkstock; 4, © Sbolotova/Shutterstock; 4–5, © Marcel Jancovic/Shutterstock; 6–7, © WaterFrame/Alamy; 8–9, © Louise Murray/Alamy; 10–11, © Alaska Stock/Alamy; 12, © Marcel Jancovic/Shutterstock; 12–13, © Stefan Wackerhagen; 14–15, © imagebroker/Alamy; 16, © Mark Raycroft; 16–17, © Rolf Kopfle/Getty Images; 18, © Sergey Lavrentev/Shutterstock; 18–19, © South West Images Scotland/Alamy; 20–21, © ventdusud/Shutterstock; 22, © Patti McConville/Alamy; 23TL, © Juniors Bildarchiv GmbH/Alamy; 23TR, © AP Photo/The Anchorage Daily News, Bill Roth; 23BL, © Dmitry Kalinovsky/Shutterstock; 23BR, © otsphoto/Shutterstock.

Publisher: Kenn Goin
Senior Editor: Joyce Tavolacci
Creative Director: Spencer Brinker
Design: Debrah Kaiser
Photo Researcher: Picture Perfect Professionals, LLC

Library of Congress Cataloging-in-Publication Data

Markovics, Joyce L., author.
    Sled dogs / by Joyce Markovics.
        pages cm. — (Bow-WOW! Dog helpers)
    Audience: Ages 5 to 8.
    Includes bibliographical references and index.
    ISBN 978-1-62724-123-6 (library binding) — ISBN 1-62724-123-X (library binding)
    1. Sled dogs—Juvenile literature. I. Title.
    SF428.7.M37 2014
    636.73—dc23
                                    2013032760

For more information, write to Bearport Publishing Company, Inc., 45 West 21st Street, Suite 3B, New York, New York 10010. Printed in the United States of America.

10 9 8 7 6 5 4 3 2 1

Contents

Meet a Sled Dog

Whoosh! I'm a **sled dog** racing through the snow.

I work with a team of other dogs.

Together, we pull a sled.

Woof! Woof!

There can be up to 20 sled dogs on a team.

Sled dogs live in cold, icy places.

The snow there makes it hard for people to get around.

So sled dogs help out!

Sled dogs have thick fur. It keeps them warm in their snowy homes.

6

The sleds we pull carry people and **goods**.

The goods include food, mail, and medicine.

The person who drives a team of sled dogs is called a **musher**.

Sled dogs do not just pull sleds for work.

We race other sled dog teams—just for fun!

The Iditarod is a famous dog sled race. It takes place every year in Alaska.

Before we set off, the musher hooks us up to our sled.

Then the musher stands on the back of the sled.

Hike!

Hike is a **command** that means "run fast."

Mushers use their voices to tell dogs where to go.

They shout "Gee" and we turn right.

They yell "Haw" and we turn left.

The dogs at the front of the team are called lead dogs. They follow the musher's commands. The other dogs follow the lead dogs.

How do puppies grow up to be sled dogs?

First, mushers train pups to pull things.

The dogs learn to drag tires around the yard.

The best sled dogs love to pull, run, and be part of a team.

The young dogs train for six to eight months.

Then they are strong enough to join a team!

Sled dogs train all year. In the summer, they pull carts.

Sled dogs dash through the snow.

They run across frozen lakes.

Nothing is better than an icy adventure!

Sled dogs can travel more than 1,000 miles (1,609 km) in one trip!

Sled Dog Facts

- A 20-dog team can pull 1,000 pounds (454 kg).

- Alaskan huskies are the most common type of sled dog.

- In 1925, a sled dog named Balto saved the lives of hundreds of sick children in Alaska. He led his team through the snow and ice to carry medicine to the kids.

A statue of Balto

Glossary

command (kuh-MAND) an order given by a person to do something

goods (GUDS) things that are bought and sold

musher (MUSH-uhr) the driver of a team of sled dogs

sled dog (SLED DAWG) a dog that is trained to pull a sled

Index

Read More

Hutmacher, Kimberly M. *Sled Dogs (Pebble Plus: Working Dogs).* Mankato, MN: Capstone (2011).

Whitelaw, Ian. *Snow Dogs! Racers of the North (DK Readers).* New York: DK (2008).

Learn More Online

To learn more about sled dogs, visit
www.bearportpublishing.com/Bow-WOW!

About the Author

Joyce Markovics lives along the Hudson River in Tarrytown, New York. She enjoys spending time with furry, finned, and feathered creatures.